AF230521

CLARA SUE KIDWELL has served as Associate Dean for Program Development at Bacone college in Muskogee, Oklahoma (2011-2013), and Director of the Native American Studies program and Professor of History at the University of Oklahoma in Norman (1995-2007). Her tribal affiliations are Choctaw and Chippewa. She received a B.A. in Letters (1962) and a M.A. and Ph.D. in History of Science (1970) from the University of Oklahoma. Before joining the faculty there in 1995 she served for two years as Assistant Director of Cultural Resources at the National Museum of the American Indian, Smithsonian Institution. Her previous teaching positions include: Associate Professor and Professor of Native American Studies at the University of California at Berkeley (1974-95), Visiting Assistant Professor in Native American Studies at Dartmouth College, Hanover, New Hampshire (1980), Assistant Professor of American Indian Studies at the University of Minnesota (1972-74), Instructor of Social Sciences at Haskell Indian Junior College in Lawrence, Kansas (1970-72), and

Instructor at the Kansas City Art Institute (1968-69). She also served as Director of the American Indian Center at the University of North Carolina at Chapel Hill (2007-2011). Her publications include *Choctaws and Missionaries in Mississippi, 1818-1918* (Norman: University of Oklahoma Press, 1995); *A Native American Theology* (Maryknoll, New York: Orbis Books, 2001), co-authored with Homer Noley and George Tinker; *Native American Studies* (Edinburgh: University of Edinburgh Press, 2005) co-authored with Alan Velie; and *The Choctaws in Oklahoma: From Tribe to Nation, 1855-1970* (Norman: University of Oklahoma Press, 2007).

NATIVE AMERICAN KNOWLEDGE SYSTEMS

CLARA-SUE KIDWELL

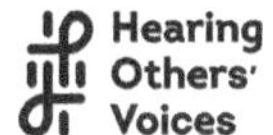

BALESTIER PRESS
LONDON · SINGAPORE

Balestier Press
Centurion House, London TW18 4AX
www.balestier.com

Native American Knowledge Systems
Copyright © Clara-Sue Kindwell, 2019

First published by Balestier Press in 2019

A CIP catalogue record for this book
is available from the British Library.

ISBN 978 1 911221 63 0

NATIVE AMERICAN KNOWLEDGE SYSTEMS

Contents

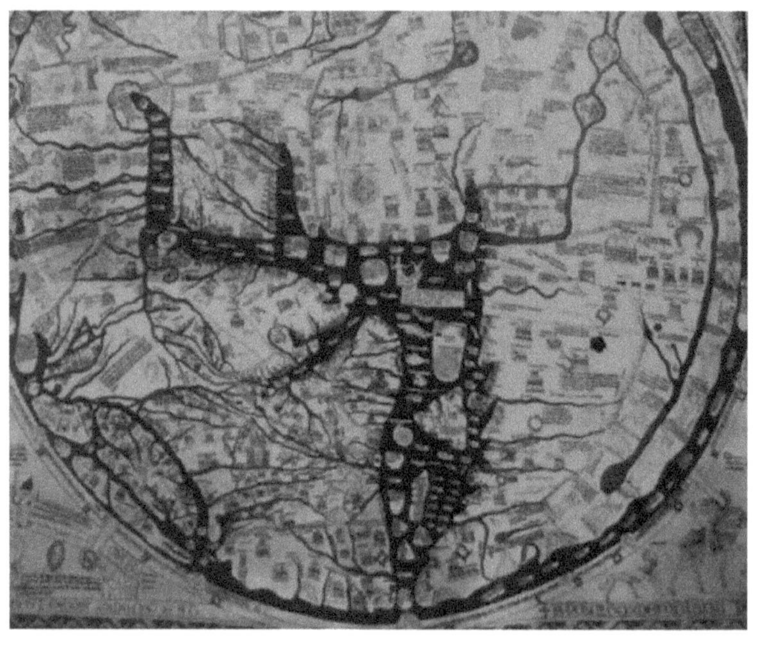

Detail from the Hereford Mappa Mundi (map of the world) 13th century

Introduction

The world is so full of a number of things,
I'm sure we should all be as happy as kings.

Robert Louis Stevenson
A Child's Garden of Verses

This simple couplet expresses one of the profound truths of the world—if we look around us, there are an immense number of separate things.

How we understand the world and our relationship to it can take many forms. This book is an attempt to explore some of the many different ways which different cultures have found to understand the physical world around them.

These ways of understanding are based on experience of the world as well as common understandings passed on from one generation to the next.

Every culture has some system of knowledge to explain its place in the world. Some of these systems are more complex than others, but each has an internal consistency based on what people have experienced. Some cultures have been characterized as "savage," or "primitive" and have been considered as inferior by other cultures. Some cultures have become highly "scientific," based on certain accepted practices of controlling their environments.

But all these systems of knowledge have allowed cultures to survive and adapt. Unfortunately, sometimes cultures do not survive. Nature can provide obstacles such as droughts, or changes in temperature, that humans cannot overcome or to which they cannot adapt. There is sufficient physical evidence of the decline of civilizations to say that not all have been successful. But it is likely that those civilizations have ways of explaining why they have not succeeded, and there is physical evidence that simply leaving one place and moving to another is a form of adaptation.

Cultures do not die completely but leave behind traces that contribute to a greater understanding of human beings and their place in the natural world.

In the 21st century there are vibrant communities of people speaking languages similar to those spoken by their ancestors in Mesoamerica thousands of years ago. Although much of the great intellectual tradition of the Mayan culture has been lost, their distant descendants still live in parts of the Yucatan Peninsula and in Guatemala, and Mayan communities are found in the United States as immigrant populations.

Looking at ways that different cultures view the world is a way of understanding different people. It is also a chance to see how systems of knowledge are formed, and how different perceptions of reality can exist. This book presents examples from cultures in Mesoamerica and North America of different ways of seeing the world. These examples may inspire readers to examine their own ways of knowing.

Mesoamerica

Mesoamerica in the nineteenth-century

Dates are important in history because history is a study of cause and effect relations. We study the past to determine what events caused other events.

We assume that what came first caused, or at least influenced, what came later. For archaeologists, who study physical remains, sequences of events are often determined by layers of remains. Those in higher layers are supposed to be more recent than those below.

In Medieval Europe, a new convention of time

keeping arose, dividing time into that before the birth of Christ, B.C., and that after the birth of Christ, In the year of our Lord, *Anno Domini*, A.D.

This convention is still widely used, although some people reject the obvious cultural bias of relating all events to the Christian god. Also, given that the birth of Christ occurred some 2,000 years ago, the designation A.D. now covers some 4,000 years and becomes unwieldy. Some writers have, however, have adopted a new convention, B.P.E., before present era, to give dates to very old events or objects. Different sources often use different conventions for designating dates.

For purposes of this study, I will try to give a time in approximate number of years from the present.

Another important distinction in terms of time is prehistoric/historic. This distinction is based upon the premise that written language is necessary to record human history. Cultures without written languages must rely upon human memory to recall past events, and human memory is not considered reliable as a source of information. Thus, many stories that are passed down for generations in societies without written languages are dismissed as myth, or legend, and are dismissed by historians, although the meaning of these traditions may take other forms of meaning, as for instance metaphors, that historians simply do not recognize.

In writing about indigenous people in North America, anthropologists have generally used the present tense, which implies that the actions being described are still being done. This use of the present tense represents the anthropologist's intent to present a "snapshot" view of cultural activities at a given point in time.

But native cultures, indeed *all* cultures, change over time, adapting to new circumstances, contact with other cultures, and new introductions of ideas and technologies. Cultural practices may change.

Native cultures are not static, however the use of the "ethnographic present," as this style of writing is called by some anthropologists, implies that they are.

A major philosophical issue in the study of indigenous cultures is the difficulty of reconciling the idea of cultural change over time (the province of historical study), and the idea that indigenous cultures exist in some unchanging state that will allow anthropologists to determine "essential" traits that characterize humans as distinct from animals or to determine the essential traits of all human cultures.

While the major cities of Western Europe, Paris, London, and Rome were still villages, native people in the valley of Mexico were building a city that was far larger than any city in Europe at the time. The site of the city, Teotihuacan, about 30 miles northeast of present-day Mexico City, was probably settled approximately 2500 years ago. it reached its height of population and influence by about 1,500 years ago, when it had a population of probably 125,000 to 200,000 people and was evidently a major trade center for towns within the basin of Mexico and probably beyond.

Teotihuacan today

The city was laid out along a major fifteen-mile-long road, designated by archaeologists as the Avenue of the Dead. There are two great pyramids, the Pyramid of the Sun and the Pyramid of the Moon, which face each other across a great central plaza, and there are distinct residential districts of the city. There are also other temples, which mark the site as a center of religious activity.

There is evidence of a fire that burned a large part of the city around 2,700 years ago. There is no evidence of outside invasion, so the fire may be evidence of internal political conflict, a civil war perhaps.

Although there is no clear evidence of who the people were who built the city, and it obviously grew over time, its population and final form influenced other peoples and cultures in the jungles and mountains of South America.

A characteristic of Mayan culture was the large buildings that served as ceremonial centers and housed large numbers of people.

Three groups of people, the Olmecs (along the coastal lowlands of the Gulf of Mexico), the Toltecs (in the Valley of Mexico), and the Zapotecs (in the Valley of Oaxaca) also left significant traces of their existence in great ceremonial centers.

These people are known primarily for the physical remains of their buildings, which have been explored by archaeologists. But they also had certain characteristics that are associated with a civilization that archaeologists have come to call Mesoamerican and that, despite differences in geography, language, and resources, came to characterize all the civilizations of the region of Central America known as Mesoamerica.

These characteristics were urbanism, social organization into a ruling class and a working class, similar religious beliefs, extremely precise calendars, glyphic systems of writing, specialized

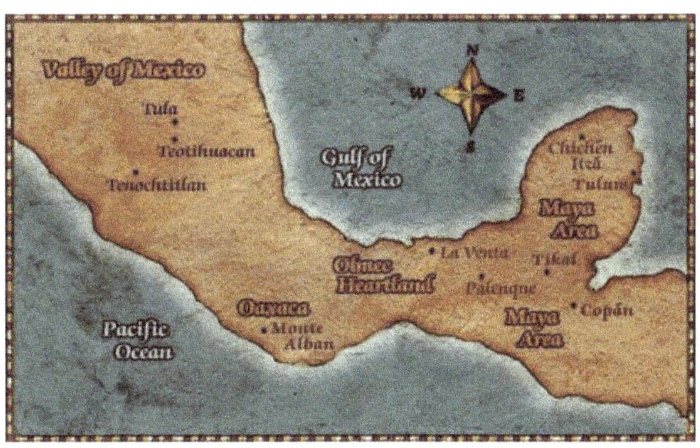

Principal culture areas of Mesoamerica

craftsmen and artisans, and similar world views. (Leon-Portillo, 1492, p. 158)

Our knowledge of these past civilizations depends primarily on the work of archaeologists who have uncovered and studied the physical remains that people from the past have left behind. Although scholars have made great progress in deciphering the hieroglyphic writing of the Mayan culture, disagreements over interpretation of physical remains indicates that the finding of archaeologists must entail a large degree of informed guesswork.

Monte Alban, for example, (a site located on the Gulf of Mexico) is interpreted by some scholars as an Olmec site, and by others as a Zapotecan site. The disagreement is important because it indicates that the same physical remains may be interpreted differently.

Monte Alban is nevertheless significant because of the urban nature of the civilization that built it.

It has a central ball court, perhaps showing that the builders were the first to play the ball game that characterized subsequent Mesoamerican civilizations. Also, carvings at the site have been interpreted as the earliest form of writing, although no one has been able to decipher its meaning.

Civilizations such as the Olmec have generally been defined by archaeologists based on assemblages of physical artifacts. The Olmec culture, for example, has been distinguished by an art style of large, carved heads.

Although Monte Alban has been differently interpreted by different scholars, it certainly shows that its builders had a very sophisticated culture that was flourishing about 5,000 years ago.

Whether the Olmec were the originators of cultural ideas that were widely adopted by other Mesoamerican cultures, it is clearly the case that in Mesoamerica high cultures existed that left physical remains which indicated a complex and sophisticated understanding of the physical world.

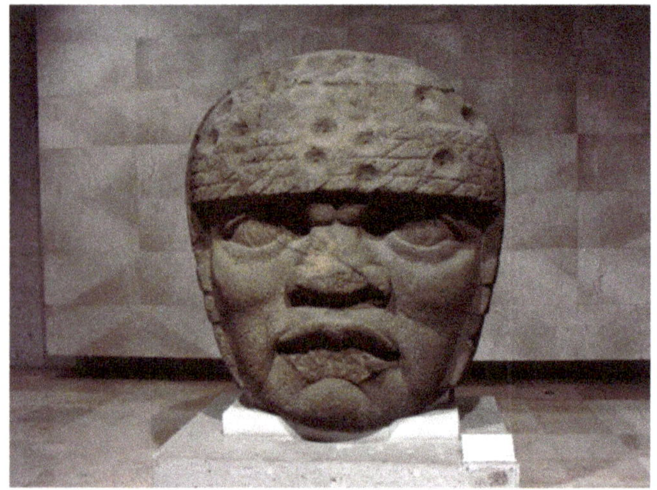

Olmec head

Two Great Civilizations of Mesoamerica

The Mayan and the Aztec, and the Incan culture of the Andes mountains have been studied because there are historical records of their intellectual traditions that are accessible to scholars, and they offer the most widely known examples of cultural development in Mesoamerica.

The Mayan culture had perhaps the most sophisticated systems of writing and mathematics and calendars of any of the Mesoamerican cultures.

The sky above is the most obvious example of the multitude of objects in the world. The sky is also the source of the most important evidence of regularity in nature—the rising and setting of the sun and the various phases of the moon are cycles that are important to humans.

But there are cycles that are less apparent but that had great significance for the Mayans. It is easy to observe day and night. Any individual can do that. But to observe solstice points, when the sun reaches its extreme point as its rising and setting points more across the horizon is not the work of a single individual. It took cumulative observations over years and probably over generations for people to realize that it always reaches the same point before reversing its course.

One of the great achievements of the Mayan culture was to note the cycles in the movements of heavenly bodies and to recognize their significance in the lives of human beings.

Mesoamerica was home to many different groups of people who interacted in different ways; some cultures flourished while others died out. The Mayan culture was probably an amalgamation of people from many different groups who spoke similar languages based on the Nahuatl language.

The Mayan civilization evidently began its evolution approximately 3,500 years ago. The main period of its intellectual development was during the classic period, generally dating from approximately 1,700 years ago to approximately 1,000 years ago.

At its height, the Mayan civilization occupied the Yucatan Peninsula, (the highlands of what is now Guatemala), and what is now Belize and Western Honduras. After flourishing for approximately 800 years, Mayan populations abandoned their major ceremonial centers. Archaeologists do not agree on the cause of the sudden decline. Perhaps foreign invasions, civil wars or natural disasters such as prolonged drought leading to widespread famine caused Mayan people to abandon some of their most remarkable achievements

One of the Mayan achievements that has been extensively studied is the calendar system that was one of the high points of the classic period. Mayan scholars were aware of and recorded extremely long cycles of movement of heavenly bodies. Heavenly bodies move relative to each other in space, but those movements are important in the lives of people on earth—the cycle of day and night, and the seasons of the year depend upon relative positions of the sun and the earth as the earth circles the sun.

Solstices and equinoxes mark the positions of the earth relative to the sun at various times of the year. The fact that the earth takes about 365 and

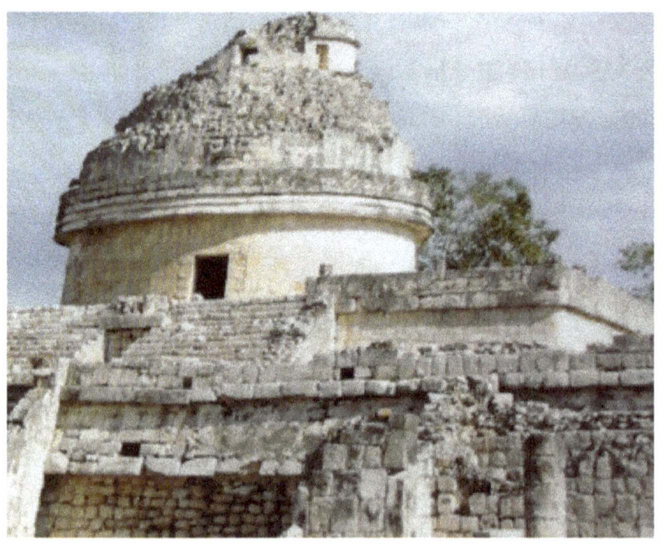

Mayan observatory, still standing in Chichén Itzá

a quarter days to complete its orbit around the sun, i.e., to return to the exact point from which it started relative to the sun, means that calendars must be periodically adjusted if they rely on a strict 365-day "year." The modern calendar inserts a leap year (with an extra day) to correct the calendar.

The Mayan civilization actually had two calendars, one based on the solar year except that it had 360 days in the year, and twenty named months, and then an additional five days of ceremonial activities. It did not correct with additional days and was known as the Vague Year since it did not always correspond exactly with the seasons, so that wintertime might occur at the beginning of a year rather than at the end.

The second calendar that the Maya followed was composed of 260 days, thirteen named days and twenty months. It was thus similar to the modern month, which has thirty or thirty-one numbered days and seven named days that repeat throughout the month.

This second calendar was like an astrological system—certain days and months had a positive influence on individuals born then, while other days and months had negative influences. The day of a person's birth could also bestow certain personal characteristics. Each day of the 260-day calendar had a unique name and number, as did the 365-day calendar, so every individual could identify the exact day of his or her birth.

The 260-day calendar was unique to the Maya, and its origin is still a matter of scholarly debate. 260 days is the average length of human pregnancy. The passage of the sun directly overhead divided the year into 260- and 120-day intervals. Whatever its origin, the 260-day calendar was highly significant for the Mayan people. It was the one that most directly governed their daily lives.

The two Mayan calendar systems, taken together, comprised a much larger cyclic system. The two calendars have been envisioned as two gears, one

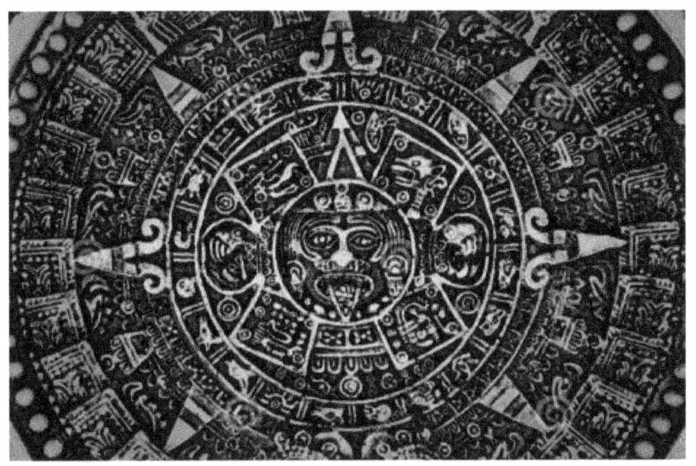

Ancient Mayan calendar

with 365 teeth and one with 260 teeth. As they turn against each other, the smaller will rotate back to the initial tooth before the larger completes its full rotation. The two teeth that started the cycle will not match up again until 18,980 uniquely named and numbered days had occurred, a total of 52 years.

This ability of the calendar to keep track of long durations of time resulted in the Long Count—a count of the number of days since a given point in past history. This linear calendar would allow the Mayans to keep track of past historically important events. Modern scholars have tried to correlate the Long Count with modern calendars but have not succeeded. The most generally accepted date for the beginning of the Long Count is 3,114 B.C. although this date has been challenged by some scholars.

The cycles of the sun are the most obvious of any in the sky. The cycle of the waxing and waning of the moon, however, occurs 13 times during the 365 day solar year, and the lunar year (the time it takes the moon to complete one circuit around the earth) is only 354 days, so the solar and lunar calendars do not correspond. Also, because of the relative positions of the earth, the sun, and the moon, there are regular periods of time that separate the occasions on which the earth's shadow blocks the sun's light from illuminating the moon, resulting in lunar eclipses.

Although eclipses appeared to be random, Mayan

scholars kept detailed records of the appearance of the moon, and one of those records contains two numbers which appear regularly, 6,585 and 177. The first number is evidently the same as the number of days that marks a cycle of eclipses that recurs regularly every 6,585 days. 177 corresponds to six lunar cycles, after which time there is a likelihood of an eclipse. Scholars have interpreted this sequence of numbers to mean that the Mayan could predict eclipses.

The Mayans also had a mathematical system, although it was evidently only used to record astronomical observations. A base twenty system may well derive from using all twenty digits (fingers and toes) of the human body as the basis for counting. Numbers were not recorded as sequences of individual marks but as series of dots and lines. Lines stood for one, and dots for five.

For example, Mayan writing, a hieroglyphic system, has been deciphered by studying patterns

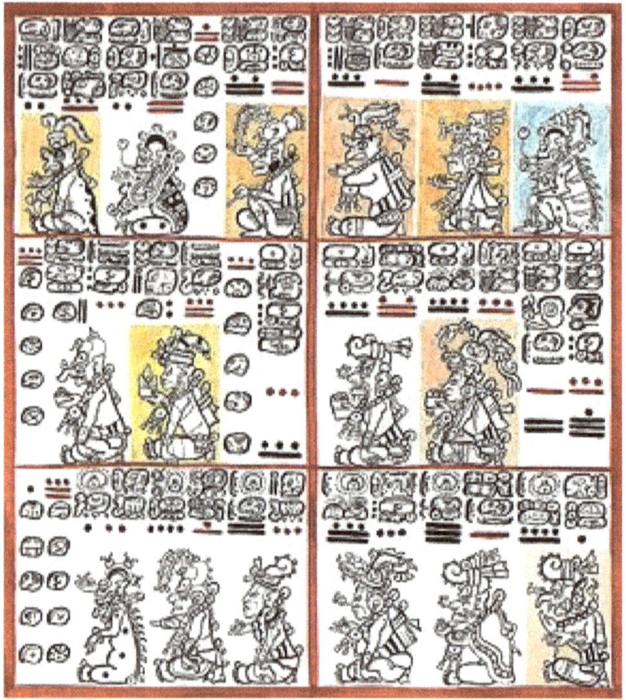

Page from codex showing Mayan number system

in carvings on temples. This writing system made possible the recording of knowledge of celestial movements on documents known as codices, which were folded rather than gathered in sheets.

With the collapse of the Mayan civilization at the end of the classic period (around 1,000 years ago) ceremonial centers were abandoned. However, their cultural remains, especially alignments of buildings to celestial phenomena, still survive to intrigue subsequent scholars. Written records of observations disappeared, except for a few isolated examples which are now preserved in museums.

A few of these codices escaped Spanish attempts to destroy all Mayan "pagan" beliefs. Mayan writing was not for literary use but rather to record on-going observations of celestial events to keep accurate calendars. Although most of the Mayan codices were destroyed, some of the knowledge that the Maya accumulated can be gleaned from the orientations of buildings.

By about the 1400's, a new population appeared in the valley of Mexico. These were the people known as Aztecs, who came as invaders from the North. They made Tenochtitlan, a settlement on a swampy island in Lake Titicaca, their capital, and it became the largest city in Mesoamerica, perhaps in the world, reaching a population of approximately 50,000 people. The Aztecs also assumed much of the knowledge of the Mayan culture, including the calendar system, which they adapted to their own needs. In Tenochtitlan they built great temples that preserved aspects of the celestial orientations that characterized Mayan sites.

The Aztecs adopted the Mayan calendar system, and in 2012 worldwide attention was focused on the Aztec calendar when it was presumed to predict the end of the world on December 21st (the winter solstice) of that year.

This prediction was based on the 52-year cycle of conjunction of the 365- and 260-day calendars. The Aztecs had built upon a cultural uncertainty regarding the Mayan cosmological interpretation of that event and practiced a ceremony intended to renew the world. The Aztec ceremony entailed the putting out of all fires in the city of Tenochtitlan and relighting them from a central fire kindled by priests in the chest cavity of a slain captive at a ceremonial site in the center of the city. The practice of human sacrifice was part of Aztec belief because their origin traditions included the belief that the sun had to be sustained by human blood.

The Aztecs believed that their world had four stages, each of which had been destroyed by conflict among their gods. The current world, the fifth, was their empire, centered in Tenochtitlan. The Aztecs controlled numerous people in areas around the city, not by military force but by trade and intermarriage. The Aztecs built floating gardens, i.e., raised beds for planting crops, by piling the rich soil from the bottom of Lake Titicaca on artificial platforms in the lake. They thus controlled trade with their subject populations, which became dependent on the city for a major part of their food and for Aztec luxury goods such as cloth, brightly colored bird feathers, and Cocoa beans.

The Aztecs also demanded tribute from their subject populations. Twenty young men and women were sent each year to the city, where they were sacrificed at a ceremonial site in the center of the city, their blood feeding the sun to sustain the Aztec world.

The Aztec calendar, and the technology of their floating gardens represented high degrees of their ability to control their natural environments. Although they have become known for the practice of human sacrifice, that practice, in their beliefs, was necessary to sustain their world.

The Inca, like the Aztecs, built a large empire. In the Andes mountains, they governed a population of approximately seven million people who occupied a territory encompassing the present countries of Colombia, Ecuador, Peru, and parts of Bolivia, Venezuela and Brazil.

This territory encompassed a wide range of

geographical conditions, from the harsh, desert-like conditions of the Atlantic coastal plains at the foot of the Andes to the highlands of the Altiplano, at an elevation of approximately 12,000 feet. The capitol city of the Incas was Cusco, in Peru, which is situated at 11,200 feet and at 23 degrees North latitude.

The Inca rulers had a very diverse terrain to deal with to build their empire. Although agriculture was difficult to develop, farmers terraced mountain slopes to control water and provide sufficient food for settled populations. One of the most dramatic achievements of the Inca was the city of Cusco itself, and the remains of their city of Manchu Picchu near Cusco (which were not discovered until 1911).

Machu Picchu shows two great examples of Incan control of environment. It has excellent examples of Incan stonework in its buildings. These are made of stacked stone carefully finished and fitted together. Because of the prevalence of earthquakes in the area, building without mortar provides a measure of stability to the buildings.

The second example is in the control of water. Because of the altitude, although the area receives abundant rainfall, the coldness of the climate creates desert conditions. The city was built with a series of catchment basins and channels that ensured that each household had sufficient water. In the city of Cusco, there are remains of an aqueduct system that channelled water down the middle of streets.

The Incas are also known for their work in gold. Small, gold plated figurines have been found in archaeological sites. Although Inca artisans valued gold and silver metals, they used them not for tools and weapons but rather for decoration and art.

The process they used involved creating an alloy of gold, silver and copper called *tumbaga*. Inca metalworkers created the gold film that they used to coat surfaces by heating and cooling the ingot. Each annealing created a thin film of gold, silver and copper oxide. The copper and silver in this film were dissolved with a paste of iron sulfate and salt. Finally, only a thin film of gold remained on the surface of the now-thin metal, which could be applied to the object being created. The gold could then be heated and burnished to produce the shiny, gold surface that characterized Andean metal work.

This technique for finishing objects created beautiful things, but it destroyed most of the precious metal of the original alloy. The resulting objects represented religious and social power for those who held them. Quechua (the main language of the Incan empire) religious texts of the 16th and 17th centuries make important use of the term *camay*, meaning the act of infusing life spirit into an inanimate object. Incan goldwork is thus not just a technological act of making an object. Gold is not important for its own sake but it infuses an object with an essential spirit.

Inca artisans were also extraordinarily skilled

weavers. Inca domesticated several animal species, especially the llama and alpaca, which were native to the Andean highlands. Their heavy fleece allowed them to adapt to the cold climate of the mountains, and they were useful to the Incas as beasts of burden and also for food.

Inca craftsmen and women became skilled in weaving fibers from the fleece of these animals and then weaving elaborate textiles. They hunted the vicuna, another native animal of the Andes, for its coat. In terms of quality, the llama has the coarsest coat, and fabric woven from its fleece was coarse and used for utilitarian garments, bags for carrying and storage, and padded armor and fabric slings for use in warfare. The alpaca has a finer coat, and garments made from its fleece were worn by individuals of higher status. The vicuna has the finest coat of all and provided the thread for the luxurious garments worn by Inca rulers. Some 125 separate shades and colors have been found in Incan textiles, evidence of a high degree of sophistication in dying techniques and knowledge of the natural plant mordant used to set the dyes.

Fibers also served as a means of *information storage* for the Incas. *Quipus* were composed of a single string, to which other strings were tied. The strings were of different colors. Each of the dependent strings might have other strings tied to it. Each string had a series of knots tied in it. The knots were tied in different patterns. The sequence of colors and patterns of knots has been interpreted as a code for information.

No one has been able to decipher the patterns. They may be strictly numerical, which means that the quipu may have been simply a record keeping system to keep track of things, which would be consistent with tracking the large amount of tribute that the Inca rulers received from the communities they conquered. Some scholars, however, maintain that the quipus were a form of writing, and that the patterns stand for words.

Fabrics may also offer clues to an Incan calendar system. A piece of cloth woven in a very complex design of circles and squares is actually two pieces woven separately then sewn together. Each of the two pieces has 10 rows of 36 circles. The diagonal rows of circles across the pieces are of different colors. The total number of circles, 365 (because

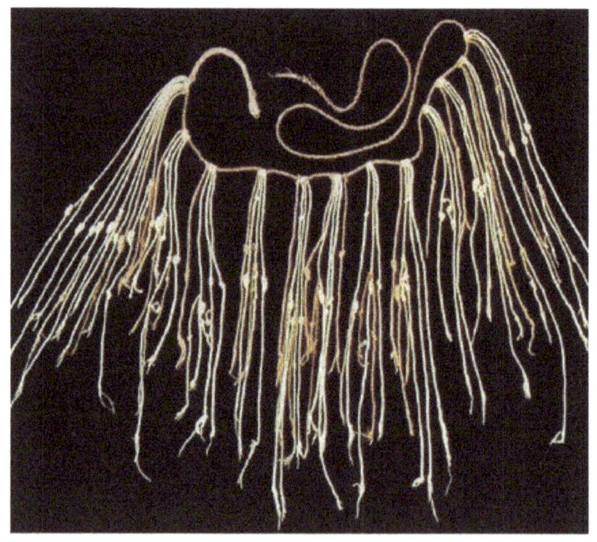

Quipu

of the diagonal pattern, some circles are counted twice) is the approximate number of days in the celestial year. Another piece of Inca fabric has a pattern of rectangles which add up to 28, near the average number of days (29.5) in a lunar month.

It thus appears that the Inca maintained a lunar calendar, based on the waxing and waning of the moon. A lunar calendar would make more sense for the Inca because the appearance of the moon varied more dramatically than did the appearance of the sun, which passes more directly overhead throughout the year at the latitude of Cusco (23 degrees from the equator). The solar year and the lunar year are different in length, but both depend upon systematic observation of celestial bodies and their positions relative to each other.

Although the position of the earth relative to the sun is important for determining seasonal cycles, for the Incas, a calendar system appears to be more important politically in determining leadership of the central government during the year. This issue is very significant since Inca government officials governed such a large and complex empire. The city of Cusco was surrounded by a series of shrines called ceques (eight) and huakas which were spaced out along lines that were centered at a point in the city of Cusco and reached to the visible horizon. The arc (the distance along the horizon) also marked the time it took the sun to travel that distance.

One theory is that the ceques and huacas were like a giant quipu dropped over the city of Cusco,

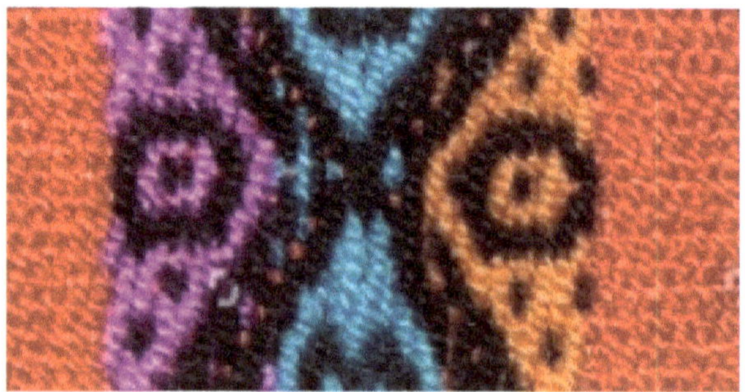

Andean textiles

and its radiating strings created the arcs, over which the sun's movement created distinct time periods. During those periods, different groups of people assumed leadership of the Incan central government.

An interesting way of thinking about the connection between celestial events and human society is that celestial events recur in cycles. What is important is that they have to recur for human societies to continue. Basing the continuation of one's society on the recurrence of celestial events is like remembering what has happened in the past, in order to predict what will happen in the future. Repetition, not change, is the most important element in the world.

One remembers the future because it has occurred in the past.

The Incas were remarkably successful as agriculturalists, given the harshness of much of their physical environment. The domestication of crops to provide a stable food supply is generally regarded as the first step leading to the concentration of populations and to the growth of cities. Indeed, textbooks often mention the "Neolithic revolution," the domestication of crops and animals in the "fertile crescent" (the valley of the Tigris and Euphrates Rivers in the Middle East).

Agriculture is generally thought to be the result of humans deliberately selecting wild plants for their desirable characteristics and then deliberately cultivating them. This interpretation leads to the view of human's dominance over plants.

Agriculture, however, can also be seen as a form of co-dependence between humans and plants. When gathering plants for their seeds, humans tend to favor plants whose seeds cling tightly to the plant. Eventually, through selection, plants lose their ability to disperse their own seeds and become dependent on humans, who must then spread the seeds by hand. Domesticated plants also have thinned seed coverings, allowing them to sprout more easily and assuring their survival. Humans learn to create suitable habitat for plants by cultivating the soil and diverting water to areas where seeds are sown.

The practices of agriculture thus make humans responsible for providing for the care and protection of plants, which happens automatically in the natural environment.

Modern potatoes descend from the variety originally domesticated in the lowlands of southern Peru and northwest Bolivia around 7-10,000 years ago (this is approximately the same time as scholars give for the domestication of corn in the highlands of Guatemala). Potatoes were originally introduced to Europe by Spaniards.

Incas also domesticated alpacas as beasts of burden and as a food source, and guinea pigs were also a small part of their domesticated food supply.

Domestication of animals depends upon certain genetic characteristic i.e., animals that tend to live in herds. The most common herd animals are sheep and goats, which thrived in the Fertile Crescent. In the Andes, alpacas had herd instincts and so could be domesticated by the Incas.

In herds there is generally one dominant animal (the alpha male). When a human can replace the alpha male so that the herd follows the human, domestication takes place. Again, the relationship is one of mutual dependence; a human takes on the role usually held by a dominant animal. Herders have to see that their flocks find appropriate feed or take on the responsibility of feeding the animals.

Domestication of animals does provide a more stable food supply than reliance on hunting wild animals. Domestication of plants and animals, however, creates new relationships of mutual dependence between humans, plants, and animals.

Inca farmers also practiced sophisticated forms of water control. They built terraced fields to trap runoff from the mountainsides. The Inca central government also collected tribute from subject populations, providing ample food for members of the nobility. In fact, *quipus* have been interpreted as recording keeping tools for such central supplies.

The Mayans, Aztecs, and Incas all had large cities, elaborate forms of civil government, sophisticated calendar systems, written languages (although these have not all been deciphered) and agricultural practices that could feed large, stable populations. They interacted with environments in complex ways.

The basic question that arises is, if left to their own devices, would these civilizations have evolved in ways that would have made them similar to civilizations of today?

This question cannot be answered in any definitive

way. We know that the Mayan peoples abandoned their great ceremonial centers about 1,000 years ago, but the cause of that collapse is not clear to modern scholars. The Aztec and Inca civilizations were overthrown by two Spanish conquerors. The Aztecs by Hernando Cortez in 1521, when Cortez overran the city of Tenochtitlan; and the Inca in 1532, when Francisco Pizzaro's army defeated an army under the leadership of Atahualpa.

Historians generally attribute the defeat of large native armies by smaller, Spanish forces to the Spanish use of iron weapons, particularly guns, and

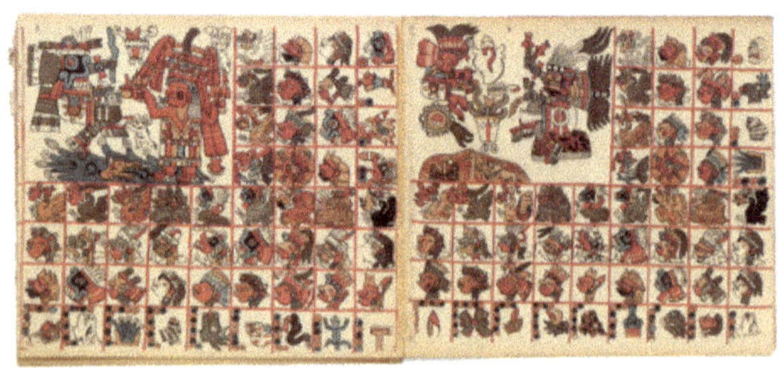

Aztec pictogram writing

horses, with which native people were unfamiliar. Europeans also introduced new diseases to which native populations had no immunity, and Christian missionaries who felt that Spanish Christianity was inherently superior to native religions, and did their best to undermine native religious leaders.

Although major Mayan religious practices had largely ceased about a thousand years ago, Mayan people still lived in the Yucatan peninsula and carried on some traditional practices. Spanish priests tried to eradicate those practices. In 1562, Bishop Diego Landa ordered a large number of Mayan codices, written in the Mayan language, to be burned, thereby destroying in a single day much of the native knowledge that had accumulated over many generations and over countless years.

Unfortunately, we will never know what further advances native civilizations in Mesoamerica might have made if left undisturbed. Archaeologists still have much to learn from numerous existing ruins in the jungles of the Yucatan peninsula, and anthropologists still find Mayan people following the indigenous calendar system in their everyday lives in the highlands of Guatemala and Chiapas.

The civilizations of Mesoamerica had ample resources to sustain themselves (although that may not have been true for the Mayans). The Aztecs and Incas had extensive trade networks. The fact that the Aztecs and Incas ruled large populations that they had been conquered by military force meant that Spaniards could easily find military allies among those subject populations to utilize against the Aztec and Inca rulers.

Indeed, Cortez took a woman from a subject tribe as his mistress. Her name was Marina. She bore him a son, the first true *mestizo* (mixed race) individual in the long history of Spanish interaction with native people in the new world. The woman (known in history as La Malinche), spoke Nahuatl, the language of the Aztecs, as well as a dialect of

Mayan, the basic language stock of many of the people the Aztecs had conquered. One of Cortez' men had been left behind on the Yucatan peninsula by a previous Spanish expedition, and had learned to speak Mayan. Marina could speak to him in Mayan, and he in turn could speak to Cortez in Spanish. Through this cumbersome (and probably confusing) linguistic process, Marina could convey information to Cortez to help him in negotiations with Aztec rulers.

The overthrow of the Aztec rulers, and the imposition of Spanish rule (with its strong emphasis on Christian belief), effectively destroyed much native knowledge and cultural practice. Indeed, Aztecs and Incas had demonstrated their ability to adapt remarkably well to the environments in which they lived, but their cultural practices were still heavily influenced by beliefs in spiritual forces in nature and a sense that humans and spirits must live in balance in order to assure the continuation of the world.

North America

In North America, native people exhibited similar diversity in languages and adaptation to a wide range of environments.

Unlike Mesoamerica, only two major population centers have been found—Chaco Canyon in what is now New Mexico, and Cahokia in Illinois, just outside the present city of St. Louis. A major question in the disciplines of anthropology and archaeology is whether culture traits can rise independently in different sites or whether they arise in one site and spread by dissemination.

This question is essentially one about human nature and the basic creativity of human beings. It is also a question about the relationship of humans and their physical environments—does adaptation to physical environments lead to similar human responses?

Throughout the world, major civilizations have arisen in major river basins or in areas dominated by water—the Chinese along the Yellow River, the Egyptians along the Nile, the ancient Sumerians in the Fertile Crescent, the Romans on the peninsula of Italy, and the Greeks on the islands of the Mediterranean Sea.

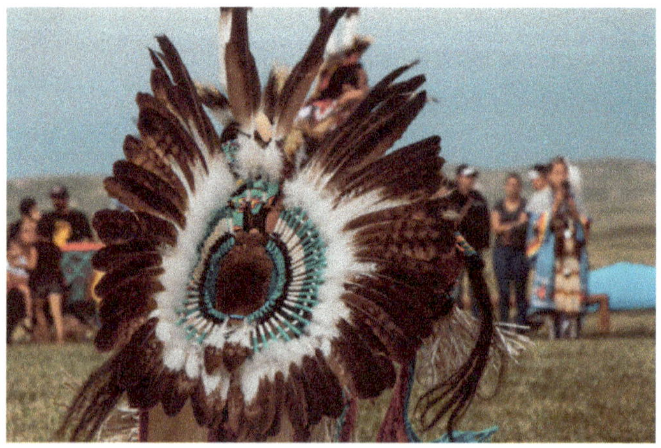

Traditional feather headdress

In North America, two major river systems exist—the Mississippi and the Missouri, but there was no corresponding growth of major centers of civilization. The most significant were Cahokia, the great mound site near St. Louis, Missouri, was near the Mississippi, and the Ancient Puebloans living adjacent to the Chaco River which runs through Chaco Canyon, in New Mexico.

In North America, for the most part native people largely remained as hunters and gatherers on the Great Plains. Corn became a staple food and was cultivated in areas where climate permitted (the northeast and southeast woodlands) but also among western peoples (the Pueblos) where an arid climate made rainfall scarce but vital to human existence.

Native people in North America also did not have domesticated animals as food sources. Buffalo and deer were major native food animals, but they did not have the genetic characteristics that made them susceptible to domestication. Although they ran in herds, they did not follow a single leader.

It is also interesting that in both Mesoamerica and North America, native people did not "invent" the wheel or use wheeled vehicles for transport. The Inca used llamas and alpacas as beasts of burden, but human energy was the main form of power for movements of materials. Even in the building of great ceremonial structures and pyramids, building blocks were moved many miles by human labor.

The two areas in which native people in North America showed the greatest skill in adapting to their environments were in agriculture and in knowledge of celestial events. Even here, corn was probably domesticated first in the Mayan territory of highland Guatemala, and introduced into North America, and the sophisticated knowledge of calendric systems among Pueblo people in the southwest is attributed by some scholars to influences from people leaving Mesoamerica and migrating to North America during the collapse of the Classic period of Mayan civilization.

The interest in and knowledge of celestial phenomena in North America may have something to do with the fact that aspects of the sky are more dramatic in northern latitudes than in the equatorial latitudes of Mesoamerica, where the sun passes more directly overhead.

It is also true that knowledge of the sky is available to all people, although not all choose to observe celestial phenomena on a regular basis, leaving that task to specialists whose knowledge is important in timing ceremonial activities.

One of the earliest sites in North America that indicates native celestial knowledge is the Bighorn medicine wheel. This medicine wheel is situated in the Bighorn mountains of Wyoming and is comprised of twenty-eight spokes radiating from a central stone cairn. Six stone cairns are positioned at irregular intervals around its perimeter. The spokes and cairns define a number of sight lines intersecting the horizon. The wheel is situated on a bluff on a mountainside at approximately 7,500 feet above the valley below, and it offers an unobstructed view of the eastern horizon.

At sunrise on the day of the summer solstice, the sight line from one of the perimeter cairns across the central cairn points directly to the rising sun. Other sight lines point to the first yearly rising immediately before dawn (known as heliacal risings) of the bright stars Rigel, Aldebaran, and Sirius. Sirius, the dog star, rises in early August and accounts for the fact that the month of August is often designated as "the dog days of summer." It makes sense to record the summer solstice day for

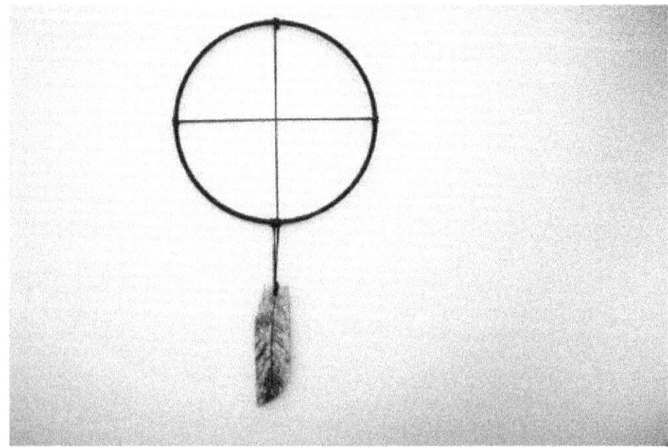

Medicine wheel orientation

people who practice agriculture, but the location of the medicine wheel puts it in the territory of ancestral peoples of the contemporary Crow and Arapahoe tribes, who were hunters, and the site of the wheel is often covered by snow on the day of the solstice because of the altitude.

The medicine wheel has also been dated (based on carbonized wood found in the central cairn) to approximately 500 years ago, which would make its construction well before the existence of contemporary tribes, and well before any practice of agriculture in the area. So why did people come to this particular site to build this particular marker?

Since it is evident that knowledge of the particular points of the sun and certain bright stars rising in the sky would have to be accumulated over years, not the work of a single individual, the existence of the medicine wheel is even more remarkable. The knowledge was not essential for daily survival, as it might have been for people who planted crops as a source of food.

So the basic question remains, why was the medicine wheel built?

One of the most dramatic examples of knowledge and marking of celestial events is at Chaco Canyon, in what is now northern New Mexico. At its height of population, about 3,000 years ago, Chaco Canyon may have had as many as 25,000 people, living in massive pueblo dwellings along the wash of the Chaco River.

The largest of these dwellings, Pueblo Bonita, backed up to a cliff and rose five stories. It had approximately 800 rooms. Although the structure is in ruins, it appears that the windows of some corner rooms were aligned to the rising of the sun on the day of the summer solstice, the only day of the year on which the sun shone directly through those windows.

The most complex alignment at the site is not in the building, but in shadows cast against the rock walls of Fajada Butte, a large butte in the canyon.

On a ledge projecting from the side of the butte, three large slabs of stone rest again the side of the butte and cast patterns of light and shadow against the wall. On the wall two spirals are carved into the surface, obviously signs of human activity and not a natural formation.

On the day of the summer solstice, a dagger of light moves downward directly through the center of one of the spirals.

Some observers might (and have) ascribed the phenomenon to simple coincidence—a random rock fall coupled with the random doodling of a bored passer-by. The position of the rocks might indeed be a random placement, but the placement of the spiral carvings, their obvious human creation, and the fact that the phenomenon occurs only once a year, on a particularly significant day, implies more than coincidence.

There are other conjunctions that happen with patterns of light cast by the sun. At the winter solstice, two daggers of light pass along the edges of the spiral. The marking of solstice points is important, but other patterns mark movements of the moon, which travels across the horizon to extreme setting points during a cycle that takes 18.6 months to complete.

Another site that shows awareness of lunar cycles is the Newark Mound site in Newark, Ohio. There, on a private golf course in the city of Newark, are outlines of a complex series of mounds, including a well-defined Great Circle and a site known as Observatory Mound. Another site is a large octagonal mound, eight sided. Sight lines along points centered on Observatory Mound along the walls of the Octagon track the movements of the moon during its eighteen-and-a-half-year cycle. An observer standing on the observatory mound would see the moon rise at the northernmost point of its 18.6-month cycle within one-half of one degree of the Octagon's exact center.

The Newark earthworks comprise the largest mound site in the world, in terms of the area covered. There are a number of other mound sites in the Ohio River valley, all of which indicate sites of particular significance to native people living in that area. The Newark earthworks are attributed to the Hopewell culture and are dated by archaeologists at approximately 1,800-1,500 years ago. They are near an assemblage of mounds in southern Ohio that include the Fort Ancient site, the great serpent mound, and various mounds in the form of animals. Although these mounds are made of earth rather than stone as are the great ceremonial mounds of Mesoamerica, they represent the efforts of large, organized groups of humans working over time.

The Newark Mounds have been studied for astronomical alignment, but there exists only speculation about other mounds in this group. These mounds are obviously of human origin, but their purpose is not clear. They obviously enclose space, and some scholars maintain that they were defensive, but the walls are not high, and there is no evidence of warfare in the region.

The question is—were they built to keep something out, or to keep something in? If they were used for ceremonial activities, it is possible that the walls were built to contain spiritual power.

One mound site (Cahokia) is a very large earthen pyramid, and there is evidence that it was the

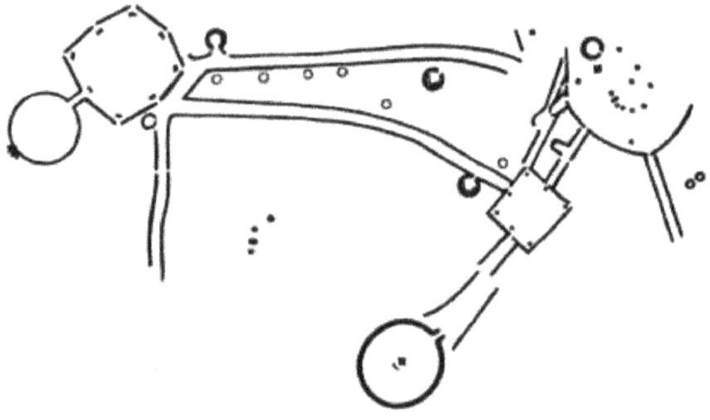

Schematic diagram Newark Mounds

center of a population concentration. It appears that a ruler, or members of a ruling group, lived on top of the pyramid. Surrounding the pyramid were communities of farmers, whose fields produced food that, in the form of tribute, sustained the rulers who lived on the pyramid.

There is an unmistakable sign of celestial orientation near the pyramid in the form of a "woodhenge," a circle of holes in the ground that once held large posts. The orientation of the posts marked solstice points, much as the stones of the famous Stonehenge in England marked solstices, or the spokes and cairns of the medicine wheel in Wyoming marked the sun's solstice rising points.

It is theorized that the ruler sighted the solstice sunrise over the "woodhenge" in order to coordinate the planting of crops in the surrounding farmland. Such an action is consistent with one of the key activities of science—the prediction of future events.

Systematic observations reveal patterns of events in the environment, and that cycles demonstrate the repetition of events in such a way as to allow people to remember the future.

Systematic observation of the environment is a hallmark of science. It also allows people to predict the future because they know what has happened in the past.

So, it is interesting that another example of the importance of uniformity in nature is in the application of a standard unit of measurement (47.5 meters, the Toltec Module) to the placement of mounds in a site in Arkansas. There are 18 mounds with a surrounding embankment spaced apart from each other by 47.5 meters (or some multiple thereof). At Cahokia, the great mound site outside St. Louis, the Toltec module seems to have been used as a basis for measurement. At the Spiro mound site is eastern Oklahoma, there is also evidence that the module was used.

In 75 percent of ancient sites in the Mississippi River Valley, there is some evidence of alignment to solar phenomena such as solstices or equinoxes, and some also show alignments to helical rising of bright stars such as Sirius. These markers confirm that the processes of nature are on-going.

If generations of observation confirm regularity in the processes of nature, why would native people continue to carry out elaborate rituals to assure that the processes go on? The reason lies in the fact that humans considered themselves part of nature and felt that their actions were part of the processes of the natural world.

The Hopi in Arizona have a ceremonial cycle that runs throughout the year. It begins (if a circle can be said to begin) with the *Soyal* ceremony, which is timed by the winter solstice. The Soyal ceremony marks the first appearance of the kachinas, who are spiritual beings who live with the Hopi during the winter season. The next ceremony, *Powamu,* takes place near the time of the winter solstice and includes the planting of beans in the ceremonial kivas, an act which obviously is done well before the actual physical planting season. At the time of the summer solstice ceremony, *Niman*, the kachina leave the Hopi villages to return to their homes in the San Francisco Mountains north of the Hopi reservation. The kachina world is considered to be a mirror image of the human world. When the Hopi are busy with the cultivation and harvesting of their own crops, the kachinas must return to their homes to plant and tend their crops.

The oral traditions of the Hopi tell that the sun is a spiritual being who travels across the sky throughout the year, from his northern house to his southern house. At these two points in his journey he would stop to rest, hence the fact that the sun at the solstices appears to rest at the northernmost (or southernmost) point of its movement across the horizon. Ceremonies performed at solstice points are perceived to give the sun the energy it needs to resume its journey.

Why are there four directions? Certainly, the rising and setting of the sun give us two directions. But the systematic observer also sees the two extreme points of the sun's path across the sky—rising higher in the sky at certain times and lower in the sky at others. These extreme points can account for two other directions.

The celebration of solstices also demonstrates an important distinction between western concepts of science, which stress experimentation to confirm natural laws, and indigenous practice which assumes that humans are part of ongoing natural processes.

The Hopi would not presume to skip a part of their ceremonial cycle to see if the sun would change its behavior as a result. To do so would risk the destruction of their own world. They would not experiment with natural processes.

Hopi farmers were also very pragmatic. After corn became a staple crop for Hopi agriculturalists, they developed a special corn seed that would grow in the arid climate of their homeland. It had a very long taproot that would grow down to reach groundwater, and a very long stem to break the soil and set the first leaves so the plant could grow. This specialized seed, along with planting techniques such as planting on banked or terraced hillsides to catch scarce rainwater, allowed the Hopi farmers to raise corn as part of their agricultural complex.

Humans were integral parts of the natural world. At San Ildefonso Pueblo in New Mexico, the ceremonial cycle was carried out by members of secret societies who gathered in sequence to pray and sing. The songs referred to events of the physical world—"bringing the buds to life," "bringing the leaves to life," and they thus presage the events of the physical world in a way that causes those events to happen in reality.

During the Chiricahua Apache girl's puberty ceremony in Arizona, marking the girl's first menses and her new status as a woman, the leader of the ceremony sings a series of songs. The ceremony is held in a tipi at night, and the singer can see the stars overhead through the smoke hole of the tipi. The singer ends his songs just as the sun begins to rise. It is said that the singer literally "pulls" the sun up over the horizon. Whether the singer is taught or knows from experience what the stars look like overhead just before sunrise, he times his performance to coincide with his observation of the stars.

Reflections on Astronomy and
Native American Knowledge Systems

It is important to understand that although all people observe the same cycles in celestial events, the way the sky looks may differ dramatically depending on the time of the year and the latitude of the observer. The 23-degree tilt of the earth's orbital plane around the sun accounts for solstices, but it also accounts for latitude.

Most people are aware that there are six months of daylight and six months of night in the arctic, but assume that day and night have the same meaning to a contemporary observer who lives in the Midwestern United States as to an Inuit person living in Barrow, Alaska. The degree of tilt of the earth's axis relative to the Sun accounts for the appearance that the sun rises higher in the sky during certain times of the year and lower in the sky during the winter. Although people may be intellectually aware of solstices, they do not observe them on a regular basis and do not appreciate the fact that the sun does not rise and set at the same points on the horizon throughout the year.

People are aware of latitude and longitude and may be vaguely aware of satellites orbiting thousands of miles above the earth that allow individuals to pinpoint their positions on the earth's surface. Latitude and longitude are essential to navigational systems.

To understand celestial phenomena, one must remember that the earth completes a journey through space around the sun in somewhat over 365 days, and that people on earth see different parts of the sky as the earth makes its journey, hence the significance of the zodiac. All the planets rotate around the sun in the same plane, although they complete their orbits in different times, and those orbits are generally parallel to the sun's plane, known as the ecliptic.

Because of the tilt of the earth's orbit, the sun's apparent path overhead varies throughout the year. Near the equator, the sun appears to move directly overhead, although it actually moves through a 23.5-degree arc. The path of the sun also appears in its rising and setting points on the horizon, which mark the solstices, the extreme points of rising and setting.

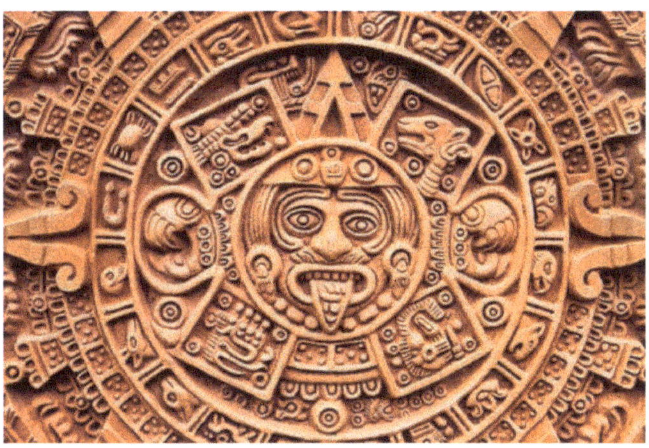

Mayan sun god

This arc of movement corresponds to the linear distance of a person's position on the earth's surface from the equator.

At the equator, latitude is 0 degrees, and at the poles, latitude is 90 degrees. At the equator, the sun appears to pass directly overhead, and at the North and South poles, and latitude is 90 degrees, the sun appears to circle the horizon. The popular concept about six months of daylight and six months of night is incorrect. For six months of winter, the sun sets lower and lower in the sky, and the environment takes on the appearance of a deepening twilight. Finally, for a period of about 30 days at the winter solstice, the sun never rises above the horizon. In summer, the process is reversed. People see the sun setting closer and closer to the horizon, until, at about the time of the summer solstice, the sun is in the sky continuously with about a month of constant daylight.

Latitude and longitude are marked with a grid of

lines on maps. The grid is like a net thrown over a globe. It is an extension of a creation by the French seventeenth-century philosopher Rene Descartes, to allow for locating objects. Ideas of latitude and longitude are creations of human beings, and they are helpful as ways of seeing the world and making sense of its meaning. Latitude and longitude are human ideas.

Time and calendar systems are based on arbitrary distinctions—why is an hour 60 seconds long? Why is a month 30 (or 31) days long? Why do we count things by 10's? Some of these things we can explain by reference to the human being—ten fingers, for example. We can explain four directions by the fact that the human body is "bilaterally symmetrical—it has a front, a back and two sides, although observation of solstice points on the horizon may also explain two additional directions.

The sky directly overhead seems filled with an uncountable array of stars. These are called "fixed stars" because they do not appear to move relative to the earth. As the earth moves around the sun during its yearly journey, it moves through different areas of the sky, and the observer on earth sees different patterns of stars.

These patterns thus constitute the Zodiac, the astrological calendar which many people believe influences human behavior or "fate." Such patterns of stars are called "constellations."

The Navajo Indians in the American Southwest recognized that the fixed stars were a background, and that there were certain patterns in those stars, although the Navajo zodiac was much different than is the contemporary one.

A story explains the origin of the fixed stars: Black God, a Navajo deity, was in his hogan (an eight-sided house with a domed ceiling inside) placing the stars carefully in patterns on the ceiling. Coyote, a mischievous figure about whom many stories were told, came in to see what he was doing. Black God looked away for a moment, and Coyote seized the buckskin bag in which Black God was keeping the stars, and he flung them upward toward the ceiling where they stuck in the seemingly random pattern that we see today.

From the story it is obvious that some Navajo observers recognized the aspect of the fixed stars.

Some of the stars seem to move relative to the fixed stars. These are the other planets in the solar system that move relative to both the earth and the sun—the planets of the sun's solar system. These are the stars that sky watchers in many cultures noted and named. For the ancient Greeks and Romans, some of those names came from the ancient gods, Mercury, Mars, Venus, Neptune. The conjunction of planets and signs of the Zodiac is the basis for the belief in astrology, that one's fate in life is controlled by the stars.

The fact that the earth's orbit around the sun takes it through the heavens and gives the earth-bound observer views of different parts of the heavens at different times of year is important for people who live by agriculture. Not all stars appear in the sky at all times of year. Some are present during only certain times, and their appearance is important as a seasonal marker, much as the solstices mark the changing of seasons.

One distinctive star group that is important for farmers is the Pleiades, a group of six bright stars and a seventh dim star. One story about the Pleiades is that a group of six brothers were out hunting one day and began chasing the largest buffalo they had ever seen. Soon they found themselves rising into the sky, following the buffalo, and they are still there. The great buffalo is the Big Dipper, and the dim star is the youngest hunter's little dog. The Pleiades disappear from the sky in the fall and reappear in the spring, and they thus define the planting season by marking the first and last killing frosts of the year.

Observation of the sky is essential to the development of agriculture—the domestication of plants so that reliable food sources will allow for the large, settled populations which can become the basis for urban life. In Mesoamerica, it is likely that ancient Mayan peoples domesticated corn approximately twelve thousand years ago in the highlands of Guatemala, and it became a staple food crop. Although corn is largely identified with indigenous peoples in North America, the first crops domesticated in North America were evidently weedy plants with significant seed heads. They volunteered in disturbed soil around native villages and would today be considered as weeds.

The oldest domesticated food plant in North America was probably the sunflower, whose tuberous root is known today as the Jerusalem artichoke (or sunchoke), and is still used as a food. There is evidence that varieties of squash were early domesticates in middle North America. In the arid southwest, bottle gourds were domesticated, dried, hollowed out, and used to carry water. Scarlet runner beans were also domesticated in the southwest. Corn did not begin to appear in native gardens in North America until approximately 2,000 years ago, well after beans and squash were established as staple crops.

How do we know what we know?

There are basically two ways of knowing—being taught, and being taught to believe what one is taught, and experiencing something directly. This idea relates to how people think about time and mark it in their languages. It may also help to explain why calendar systems are so integral to systems of knowledge.

The English language conditions people to think in terms of past, present, and future. If, however, one realizes that there are different ways to think about time, you can see how we can know through experience what has already happened, but we can only speculate about what has yet to happen. We can, however, anticipate the future based on what has happened in the past, but we cannot know the future with any real certainty.

Native languages are a key to understanding how indigenous people understood their worlds. Native languages often make a distinction between what one knows through personal experience, and what one hears from others.

The Cherokee language, for example, makes such a distinction. The Makah language uses the phrase *pa l silali* if a person has seen or experienced something directly, but the phrase *pat'si l ititwad* is used if someone has only heard about something. This distinction is so crucial that it is embedded in the very language that people speak.

In Mesoamerica scholars have found evidence of written language in Mayan inscriptions and Aztec codices. Although parts of the meaning of these languages have been understood, efforts continue to translate the meaning of these writings. In North America, these were no languages written by native people. The first native writing system was not created until 1821, when the Cherokee scholar Sequoyah created a syllabic alphabet of 86 characters to record Cherokee speech and treaty negotiations between Cherokee leaders and representatives of the United States government.

Indigenous languages in both North and South America that do not have written forms must rely upon direct, personal interaction between individuals—and another person's opinion may be subject to question. Direct, personal experience of events is the most reliable way of knowing something. Not all individuals, however, can personally experience all events in the natural environment. People's beliefs in any culture generally come from shared belief systems.

People believe things which they have not experienced directly because they recognize certain patterns in the natural environment, or certain events in human behavior.

The Chippewa of Northern Minnesota know about the Thunderbird. The Thunderbird is a great, spiritual bird whose presence takes the form of thunderstorms. The beating of its wings creates thunder and wind, and the flashing of its eyes is lightning.

Proof of the Thunderbird's existence comes from the association of birds and storms. In the spring in Northern Minnesota, prevailing wind patterns move from southeast to northwest, as birds follow their yearly migration patterns. Storms also move from southeast to northwest. This connection between the behavior of birds and of storms provides evidence for the existence of the Thunderbird as a causal agent in the coming of storms.

Another spiritual being who plays a large part in the beliefs of the Chippewa is the Windigo, the great cannibal monster who roams the woods of northern Minnesota. The Windigo is described as a great, hairy being, human-like in form, with a heart of ice and a sharp, six-inch-long nail on the big toe of his right foot. This nail is for impaling his victims. Anyone who comes into contact with the Windigo will be turned into a cannibal.

The Windigo is a very real monster. The Chippewa of northern Minnesota have adapted themselves to the very harsh environment of the area. They usually hunted in small groups, and lived in isolated family units during the winter. They depended upon hunting to survive the winter. The solitary hunter, or small group of hunters, had to brave the elements and were constantly aware that the survival of their families depended upon their ability to kill game. The animals of the northern woods were solitary—elk, moose. There was no guarantee that the hunter would be successful. The fear of starvation was real and always present.

So, the hunter, alone in the woods, surrounded by strange noises and movements in the brush, could readily fear the presence of the Windigo.

Documented evidence of episodes of cannibalism from historical newspapers show the reality of what happened when starvation became a reality. The Windigo thus becomes a metaphor for fear, isolation, and hunger. As one anthropologist put it, "The man who does not flee in terror from the presence of a Windigo is either an example of supreme intellectual emancipation, or a complete fool."

The Windigo and the Thunderbird are real beings within the experience of the Chippewa of northern Minnesota. The phenomena that they explain are very real, and experience translates into metaphorical language that makes sense of the physical world within which the Chippewa live.

A metaphor is generally defined as a word or object that replaces another word or object to create a new meaning. The Windigo, for example, comes to stand for a complex of experiences involving hunger, cold, isolation, and fear. The Thunderbird stands for wind, thunder, lightning, and fear of natural phenomena, i.e., storms.

An elaborate metaphor from the Cherokee, who were farmers in the south-eastern part of what is now the United States is the story of Selu, the Corn Mother.

The story is that Selu was feeding her family a delicious food, but she would not tell them where she was getting the food. Her twin sons decided to follow her one day, and they found her in a small hut behind the main cabin, where she was rubbing skin from parts of her body. It was falling into a basket, where it became the food she had been feeding them.

The sons thought that this was an example of witchcraft and were appalled at their mother's behavior. When she discovered that her sons had learned her secret, she told them that they must kill her and drag her body around the grounds of the cabin. They did, and the next spring they discovered corn plants growing where her body had touched the earth.

The story of Selu is an extended metaphor where Selu, the physical corn plant, encompasses femininity, nurturing, the cycles of nature, and the human cycle of life and death. The mother must die as the corn plant died after the harvest, but the corn seeds will grow again the next year, to provide food for the people.

Understanding metaphors demands an understanding of the cultural values of a people. Although Thunderbirds and Windigos may be dismissed as myths or superstitions, they are powerful ways of expressing an understanding of the physical environment within which people live. They are different but very real ways of looking at the world.

Conclusion

There are many ways of understanding the world. This book is intended to demonstrate some of the different ways that different groups of people have understood their worlds.

Throughout human history, people have created systems and observed relationships in natural phenomena that have tried to explain the nature of "reality." In ancient Greece, followers of the philosopher Plato maintained that the reality of the physical world existed only in the minds of humans as ideas that they were born with. This philosophy of "idealism" meant that humans recognized a reality in the world around them because they had innate ideas in their minds when they were born.

On the other hand, followers of the philosopher Aristotle maintained that humans could recognize similarities among things and classify them into groups. All chairs, for instance, no matter how different in shape or material, shared similar functions, and they thus constituted a particular reality.

In studies of native languages, scholars have found different expressions of reality. The Hopi, a Puebloan people whose homeland is in central Arizona, express their understanding of their reality in terms of "anticipation of the heart." Their world is constantly manifesting itself. The Hopi thus anticipate that reality is constantly coming into being, and if the Hopi remain of good heart in their beliefs and behavior, their world will continue. The same is true for the Wintu people of Northern California.

Some of these groups of people no longer exist. Some do, but they live much differently than their ancient ancestors did and understand their worlds differently.

Their ideas remain and deserve our respect and study, a way of knowing to learn from.

You might also like ...

If you enjoyed this, you might also like some of the following:

Internet links:

http://www.ancient-wisdom.com/olmecs.htm/
https://en.m.wikibooks.org/wiki/The_History_of_the_
Native_Peoples_of_the_Americas/Mesoamerican_
Cultures/

Books:

Clara Sue Kidwell, *A Native American Theology*, Orbis Books, 2001.
Alfonso Ortiz and Richard Erdoes, *American Indian Myths and Legends*, Pantheon, 1990.
Ray A Williamson, *Living the Sky: Cosmos of the American Indian*, University of Oklahoma Press, 1987.

Or, for the future (perhaps)

https://www.sciencebuddies.org/science-engineering-careers/

https://aas.org/learn/careers-astronomy

https://www.discoveranthropology.org.uk/career-paths.html/

Questions for discussion, reflection, and action

Ask some of your friends how they know what they know? or your teacher? or yourself? What evidence are you relying on? Do you think others (who?) might see it differently?

How important is the sun for understanding our lives? our way of thinking? knowledge systems? science?

Do you think there are any similarities here to ways of thinking in medieval Europe and/or in the ancient classical world?

Did any of the book's accounts of astronomy surprise you? If so in what way and why? Is there anything to learn from this different way (if it is different) of understanding the skies and its bodies?

Set up a debate (within yourself if no one else is at hand but best if you can have two sides) with one side supporting, the other opposing, the idea that Native American knowledge systems should be called 'science.' Does the outcome matter? (why or why not)?

Does any of the account in this book link up with other of your academic or non-academic interests? If so why (or why not) and in what way(s)? What are you planning to read next?

If someone asked you what (if anything) you personally had gained from this book what might you say? Or your friends? (if the answer is 'nothing' the reason for that might be interesting to explore too.)

NOTE: The publishers wish to express their gratitude to the many internet sites that display free, non-royalty, and downloadable images, especially the most generous photographers in the world who give their photos free to the wonderful 'unsplash' resource.

Hearing Others' Voices: A transcultural and transdisciplinary book series in simple and straightforward language, to inform and engage general readers, undergraduates and, above all, sixth formers in recent advances in thought, unaccountably overlooked areas of the world, and key issues of the day.